Customize your Clothes

Molly Perham

LORENZ BOOKS

This edition is published by Lorenz Books, an imprint of Anness Publishing Ltd
Hermes House, 88–89 Blackfriars Road, London SE1 8HA
tel. 020 7401 2077; fax 020 7633 9499

www.lorenzbooks.com; www.annesspublishing.com

If you like the images in this book and would like to investigate using them for
publishing, promotions or advertising, please visit our website
www.practicalpictures.com for more information.

© Anness Publishing Ltd 2009

UK agent: The Manning Partnership Ltd; tel. 01225 478444; fax 01225 478440;
sales@manning-partnership.co.uk
UK distributor: Grantham Book Services Ltd; tel. 01476 541080; fax 01476 541061;
orders@gbs.tbs-ltd.co.uk
North American agent/distributor: National Book Network; tel. 301 459 3366;
fax 301 429 5746; www.nbnbooks.com
Australian agent/distributor: Pan Macmillan Australia; tel. 1300 135 113; fax 1300 135 103;
customer.service@macmillan.com.au
New Zealand agent/distributor: David Bateman Ltd; tel. (09) 415 7664; fax (09) 415 8892

Publisher: Joanna Lorenz
Editorial Director: Judith Simons
Editor: Molly Perham
Photographers: James Duncan, John Freeman, Anthony Pickhaver
Designer: Alix Wood
Jacket Design: Balley Design Associates
Production Controller: Claire Rae

ETHICAL TRADING POLICY
Because of our ongoing ecological investment programme, you, as our customer,
can have the pleasure and reassurance of knowing that a tree is being cultivated on
your behalf to naturally replace the materials used to make the book you
are holding. For further information about this scheme, go to
www.annesspublishing.com/trees

PUBLISHER'S NOTE
Although the advice and information in this book are believed to be accurate and true
at the time of going to press, neither the authors nor the publisher can accept any
legal responsibility or liability for any errors or omissions that may be made.

Acknowledgements

The projects in this book were created by Petra Boase, Marion Elliott,
Cecilia Fitzsimmons and Jacki Wadeson.

Contents

Introduction......................................4

TERRIFIC T-SHIRTS
Birthday Present 8
Bug Collector.........9
Noughts & Crosses ..10
Disco Dazzler 11
Muddy Puppy....................12
Really Wild 14
Spots and Dots 15
Pockets of Fun 16
Crazy Spiral 17
Hungry Cat 18
Hawaiian Dancer..................20
Space Trekker 21
Fruity T-shirt & Shorts 22
Flower Power Leggings......23

FASHION ACCESSORIES
Appliquéd Scarf 26
Wintry Gloves & Scarf.......27
Fancy Gloves.......................28
Pompom Hat........................29
Stamped Scarf....................30
Bug Socks 31
Doodle Print Shoes........32
Sunglasses Strap.....33
Clay Fish 34

Papier-mâché Cat...............35
Birthday Badge...................36
Button Heart 37
Happy Face.........................38
Paper Flower 39

JAZZY JEWELLERY
Rolled-paper Beads............42
Leafy Jewellery...................43
Jungle Bracelet 44
Knotty Necklace 45
Stripes & Beads Bracelet ..46
Buttons & Beads 48
Heart & Star Rings 49
Christmas Tree Earrings....50
Star Brooch & Earrings 51

FUNKY HAIR
Sponge-flower Hairband 54
Hippy Headband..................55
Striped Beaded Barrette...56
Glitzy Hairband..................57
Special Scrunchie 58
Braided Flips 59
Christmas Hair Slides .60
Hair Wrap................61
Braiding Fun.............62
Index...................64

Introduction

If you customize your clothes it means that you will never look exactly like everyone else. T-shirts, socks, gloves, scarves and hats can all be decorated in your own individual style. You can also make stylish jewellery, badges and hair accessories.

Painting T-shirts is such good fun that once you have tried it, there will be no stopping you. In this book you will find designs for both short- and long-sleeved T-shirts. Choose cotton T-shirts, and if you are using a new one, it is a good idea to wash and rinse it to remove any excess dye. When the T-shirt is dry, ask an adult to iron it to smooth out creases. It is always a good idea to insert pieces of stiff card (stock) into the body and sleeves, to prevent fabric paint from seeping through the T-shirt. And remember that fabric marker, like fabric paints, cannot be washed out – so practise your designs on a piece of paper before drawing directly on to the T-shirt.

Stamping is another way of decorating your T-shirts, as well as leggings, shorts and other items of clothing. You can buy wooden or rubber stamps, or make your own individual designs using cardboard, a sponge or a potato. Whether using ready-made stamps or your home-made ones, wash them gently after use, and in between each print when you are using a different coloured ink.

To customize scarves, gloves and hats, you can experiment with pieces of felt, brightly-coloured threads, buttons and beads. Or try making a stylish pompom hat from an old pair of wool tights and scraps of knitting wool. Badges are easy to make and great fun to wear. As well as wearing them on your clothes, you could jazz up a hat or bag. Always make sure the badge pin is fastened securely, or your badge might fall off. All kinds of materials can be used for badges. In this book you will find ideas for making badges with clay, papier-mâché, pipe cleaners and crêpe paper.

Making your own customized jewellery is a great way of creating an individual style. Embroidery thread makes really colourful necklaces and bracelets – choose a colour scheme that matches your clothes, or goes with a particular theme. You can knot your favourite beads into the threads, or even make your own beads from the pages of a magazine. Rings, brooches and earrings will complete your collection of jewellery.

There are lots of things you can do to your hair to give an outfit a whole new look. Make an eye-catching hairband, slide or scrunchie to match your favourite clothes. Or create a stunning new hairstyle – all you need is a brush and comb, and a selection of brightly coloured ribbons, beads, cord and covered bands. First, practise how to do a simple braid and ponytail, as these form the basis of many styles. It's great if you have a friend to help – then you can do each other's hair.

The projects in this book are all fun and easy to do. Once you have managed the basics, let your imagination run wild and create your own masterpieces.

Decorating T-shirts with fabric paints, threads and material is fun and very easy to do. In no time at all you will be creating stylish and wacky T-shirts for yourself, friends and family. Here you will find T-shirt designs for bug collectors, animal lovers, space trekkers and disco dancers.

Terrific T-Shirts

Birthday Present

Why not make this T-shirt as a gift for a friend's birthday? They could wear it to their own party! It is important that the painted ribbon is identical to the real ribbon. To achieve this, you may have to mix fabric paints together to make exactly the right colour.

YOU WILL NEED

- Large sheet of card (stock)
- Short-sleeved T-shirt
- Ruler
- Fabric marker pen
- Container of water
- Fabric paint (green, white, pink)
- Medium and thick paintbrushes
- 40–50cm (16–20in) of wide, white-spotted green ribbon
- Scissors
- Green sewing thread
- Sewing needle

1 Insert card (stock) in the body and sleeves. Use the ruler and marker pen to draw two lines down the centre and across the T-shirt, the width of the ribbon.

3 Use the medium brush to decorate the painted ribbon with small dots of white fabric paint. Wash the brush. Cover the rest of the T-shirt with larger pink dots. Allow to dry.

2 ▲ Paint the area inside the lines with green fabric paint. Do this with the thick brush. These are the ribbons on the present. Make the edges of the ribbon as straight as possible. Allow to dry.

HANDY HINT
Try adding a little water to a fabric paint – it makes the paint easier to apply and changes the colour slightly. Do not make it too runny or it will drip.

4 ▲ Tie the length of ribbon into a big bow. Trim the ends. Thread the needle with thread and tie a knot in the end. Position the bow where the painted ribbons cross and sew it into place. Keep sewing until the bow is securely fixed.

Bug Collector

Aargh! Don't look now but there are spiders and insects crawling all over you. The Bug Collector T-shirt is not for the squeamish – it is for the enthusiastic mini-beast collector who really wants to bug friends and family. You can invent your own creatures, or better still, copy them from real life!

YOU WILL NEED

- Large sheet of card (stock)
- Long-sleeved T-shirt
- Fabric marker pen
- Container of water
- Fabric paint (black, red)
- Fine and medium paintbrushes
- Black fabric paint or iridescent fabric paint in squeezy containers

1 Insert pieces of card (stock) inside the body and sleeves of the T-shirt. Use the fabric marker pen to draw three large spiders on the front of the T-shirt. Draw two or three spiders on each sleeve.

2 ▶ Use the medium brush and black fabric paint to paint the spiders' heads, bodies and antennas. To paint the black jointed legs, use the fine paintbrush. Allow to dry.

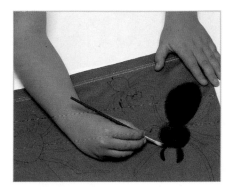

3 Wash the paintbrushes in water and use the fine paintbrush to paint the spiders' eyes red.

4 Dip a finger into the black fabric paint and press it on to the T-shirt to make the body and head of a small insect. Repeat to make more mini-beasts. Allow to dry.

5 ▲ To paint legs on the small bugs, use black fabric paint or iridescent fabric paint in squeezy containers. Allow the paint to dry. Paint more bugs on the back of the T-shirt.

HANDY HINT

Make a spider stamp with a halved potato. Etch the shape into a cut surface of the potato. Cut around the shape, dip the stamp into fabric paint and press it on to the T-shirt.

9

Noughts & Crosses

This T-shirt board game is also known as tic-tac-toe.

YOU WILL NEED

- 2 sheets of card (stock)
- Short-sleeved T-shirt
- Ruler
- Fabric marker pen
- Iridescent fabric paint (orange)
- Pencil
- Scissors
- Blue and red felt
- Fabric glue
- 9 sticky-back hook--and-loop dots

1 ▶ Insert a piece of card (stock) inside the body of the T-shirt. Use a ruler and fabric marker pen to measure and draw the Noughts and Crosses grid. The lines should be 24cm (10in) long and 8cm (3in) apart.

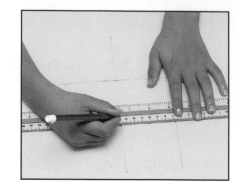

2 ◀ Go over the lines with orange iridescent fabric paint in a squeezy tube. Move the tube evenly along the lines or the paint will form blobs. Allow the paint to dry.

3 ▶ To make templates for the noughts and crosses, draw an X and an 0 on a piece of card and cut them out. Place the templates on to the felt and draw around them. You will need four red noughts and four blue crosses. Cut out the shapes. Cut out four small blue ovals and glue on to the noughts with fabric glue.

4 ▲ Remove the backing from the hook-and-loop dots and press one loop half of each dot into the centre of each square. Press one hook half on to the back of each shape. You are now ready to play Noughts and Crosses!

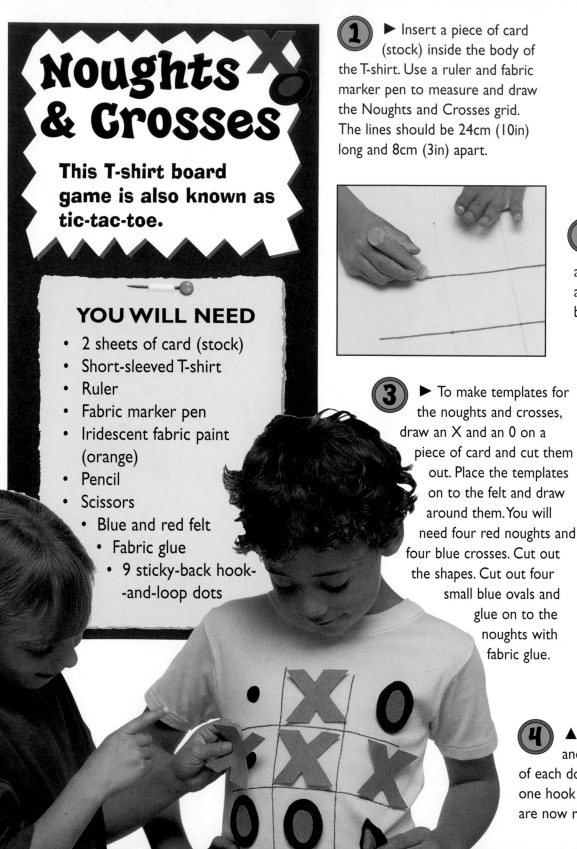

Disco Dazzler

Wear this wild T-shirt to be the centre of attention. The patterns will glow in the dark under ultraviolet light because they have been painted using fluorescent fabric paint.

YOU WILL NEED

- Large sheet of card (stock)
- Short-sleeved black T-shirt
- Chalk fabric marker
- Container of water
- Fluorescent fabric paint (yellow, blue, pink, orange, green)
- Medium paintbrush
- Puffa fabric paint (orange, yellow, purple, red)
- Hairdryer

(1) ▼ Insert pieces of card inside the T-shirt. Use the chalk fabric marker to draw the outlines of triangles, spirals and zigzag patterns all over the front and the sleeves.

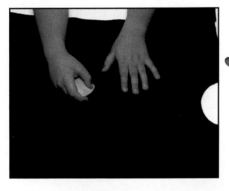

(2) ▲ Use fluorescent yellow, blue, pink, orange and green fabric paint to fill in the outlines. You can even mix the colours together. Allow the fabric paint to dry.

(3) Decorate the T-shirt with dots and squiggles of orange, yellow, purple and red puffa fabric paint. To make the puffa paint puff up, dry it with a hairdryer set on cool.

(4) Decorate the bottom of the T-shirt with a zigzag pattern, using puffa fabric paint. Once again, use the hairdryer set to its coolest temperature to dry the puffa paint.

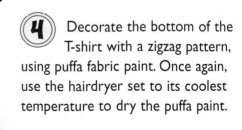

11

Muddy Puppy

Oh, no! Someone has let the puppy walk all over this T-shirt with its muddy paws! Surely such a naughty puppy does not deserve to be given a big, juicy bone! To stop the puppy covering everything with mud, it has been given a fancy pair of socks to wear. Give it a ribbon bow to match the socks.

1 ▼ Insert pieces of card (stock) inside the body and sleeves of the T-shirt. Draw a dog on a piece of card and cut it out. Place the template on the front of the T-shirt. Draw around it using the fabric marker pen.

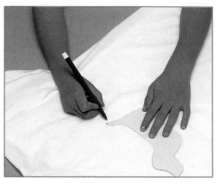

YOU WILL NEED

- 2 sheets of card (stock)
- Short-sleeved T-shirt
- Pencil
- Scissors
- Fabric marker pen
- Container of water
- Fabric paint (brown, black, white, red, blue, yellow)
- Fine and thick paintbrushes
- Narrow yellow ribbon
- Fabric glue and brush
- Sponge

2 ▼ Paint the dog brown using the thick brush. If you do not have brown paint, make some by mixing together blue, red and yellow. Make light and dark shades of brown by adding white or black. Allow the paint to dry before starting the next step.

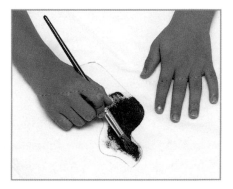

3 ▼ Use the fine brush to paint black spots on the dog's body. Continue using the black paint to paint the dog's ear, tail, shoes and a bone. Add features to the face and decorate the socks and the shoes. Paint a colourful collar.

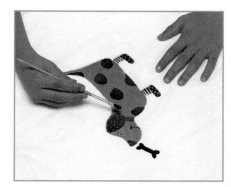

4 ▼ Let the paint dry before starting this step. Tie the piece of ribbon into a small bow. Trim the ends. Fix the bow on to the collar with fabric glue. Hold the bow in position until the glue is dry.

5 ▼ To make a stencil, draw the outline of a paw print on a piece of card. Use scissors to snip into the middle of the outline. Cut out the stencil following the outline. Turn the T-shirt over so that the back is facing you. Make sure that the pieces of card are still in position inside the T-shirt.

6 ▼ Place the stencil on the back of the T-shirt. Hold it in position and use a sponge to dab light and dark brown fabric paint on the stencil. Lift off the stencil carefully. Repeat this several more times until the back of the T-shirt is covered all over with muddy paw prints.

13

Really Wild

It's time to go on safari, but you must tread softly so that the real Kings of the Jungle do not see you! Lions and tigers may not like you prowling on their territory.

YOU WILL NEED

- Large sheet of card (stock)
- Long-sleeved T-shirt
- Fabric marker pen
- Container of water
- Fabric paint (brown, red, orange, yellow, black)
- Thick paintbrush

1 ▶ Insert a piece of card (stock) inside the body of the T-shirt. Use the fabric marker pen to draw the outlines of the tiger stripes on the front of the T-shirt.

2 Paint the stripes using brown, red, orange, yellow and black fabric paints. It does not matter if the stripes are uneven as this will make them look more realistic.

3 When the paint is dry, turn the T-shirt over. Check that the card is still in place inside. Use the marker pen to draw more stripes and a tail on the back of the T-shirt.

4 ▲ Use the same colours as before to paint the stripes and tail. Allow the paint on your Really Wild T-shirt to dry before you start growling and prowling around in it.

Spots and Dots

This is the perfect T-shirt to wear when you are out with your friends. The design is very simple to draw and you can use as many or as few colours as you like.

YOU WILL NEED

- Large sheet of card (stock)
- Short-sleeved T-shirt
- Fabric marker pen
- Container of water
- Fabric paint (red, black, pink, blue, white)
- Medium paintbrush
- Puffa fabric paint (purple, red, yellow, orange, blue)
- Hairdryer
- Glitter fabric paint (silver)

1 Insert pieces of card (stock) inside the body and sleeves of the T-shirt. Use the fabric marker pen to draw large circles on the front of the T-shirt. Draw some circles on to the sleeves as well.

HANDY HINT

When using puffa or glitter fabric paints in squeezy containers, always keep the nozzle moving smoothly over your design. If you let the nozzle rest, the paint will form blobs.

2 ◄ Use the medium brush to paint the circles different colours. Remember to wash the brush when changing colours. Allow the fabric paint to dry before starting the next step.

3 Use purple, red, yellow, orange and blue puffa fabric paint to decorate some of the circles with swirls, lines and spots. To make the paint puff up, dry it with a hairdryer set on cool.

4 ◄ To make your T-shirt more dazzling, decorate the remaining circles with silver glitter paint. To finish, add glitter paint to those circles already decorated with puffa fabric paint.

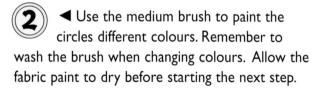

15

Pockets of Fun

When you wear this T-shirt, you will no longer lose or leave at home your pocket money. You could also use the pockets for carrying other valuable things.

1 ▶ Cut three pockets and three decorative strips from the orange, mauve, green and blue felt. The strips must be long enough to fit along the top edge of each pocket. Glue a strip on to the top of each pocket with fabric glue.

2 Position the pockets along the bottom of the T-shirt with pins. Thread the needle and tie a knot in the end. Use thread that is a different colour from the pocket. Sew the pockets on to the front of the T-shirt, using big stitches.

3 ◀ Use the fabric pen to draw outlines of sweets (candy), coins and dice above each pocket. You could also draw pencils, jewellery, sunglasses and hair clips.

HANDY HINT
Place a piece of card inside the body of the T-shirt when sewing on the pockets. This will stop you from sewing the front and the back of the T-shirt together!

4 Insert a piece of card into the body of the T-shirt. Paint the sweet (candy) wrappers and dice in bright colours. Use gold fabric paint for the coins. When the paint is dry, fill the pockets with all your treasures!

16

Crazy Spiral ◎

If you are new to fabric painting this design is easy to do. Draw the outline of the spiral as big as you can to make it easy to decorate. You can add smaller spirals to the design or paint a spiral on to the back of your T-shirt, too.

YOU WILL NEED

- Short-sleeved T-shirt
- Large sheet of card (stock)
- Fabric marker pen
- Container of water
- Fabric paint (black, orange, yellow, light blue, green)
- Fine, medium and thick paintbrushes
- Iridescent fabric paint (yellow, orange, purple)
- Glitter fabric paint (green, purple)

1 ► Insert pieces of card inside the body and sleeves of the T-shirt to prevent the paint from seeping through. Use the fabric marker pen to draw a large curly spiral on to the front of the T-shirt.

2 ◄ Paint the spiral with black fabric paint using the thick brush. Allow the paint to dry, then decorate the spiral with coloured dots. Do this with the medium brush.

3 Draw circles around some of the dots using yellow iridescent fabric paint. Go around the outline of the spiral with orange and purple paint. Leave to dry.

4 ▼ Make dots of yellow iridescent fabric paint inside the spiral. Use glitter fabric paint to cover the front of the T-shirt with green dots. To finish, dot the sleeves with purple glitter paint.

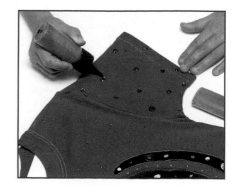

Hungry Cat

This Hungry Cat is dreaming of a seafood feast. If the dream does not come true, the cat's contented purr will become a moaning miaow. Does the cat get its wish? Look at the back of the T-shirt to find out. Oh dear, poor little fish!

YOU WILL NEED

- 2 sheets of card (stock)
- Short-sleeved T-shirt
- Pencil
- Scissors
- Fabric marker pen
- Container of water
- Fabric paint (blue, white, black, red, yellow, orange, pink)
- Medium and thick paintbrushes
- Sponge
- Black embroidery thread
- Embroidery needle

1 ▲ Insert a piece of card (stock) inside the body of the T-shirt. Draw a cat's head on another piece of card and cut it out. Place this template on the front of the T-shirt and draw around it with the fabric marker pen.

18

2 ► Use the thick brush to paint the cat's face with blue-grey fabric paint. To make this colour, mix blue, white and black fabric paints together. Let the paint dry, then paint the eyes, nose and insides of the ears.

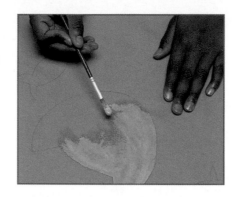

3 ► Draw five fish using the fabric marker pen. Use the medium brush to paint the fish different colours. This hungry cat is dreaming of its fish lunch, so give it a happy and contented face. Paint and decorate the cat's fancy collar. Allow the paint to dry.

4 ◄ To make a stencil, draw the outline of a fish skeleton on a piece of card. Use scissors to snip into the middle of the outline. Cut out the stencil following the outline. Place the stencil on the back of the T-shirt and dab it with a sponge dipped in red paint. Lift off the stencil. Stencil four more skeletons in different colours.

5 ► When the fabric paint is dry, remove the card and turn the T-shirt over again. Thread the needle with black embroidery thread and tie a knot at the end. Sew four long stitches on either side of the cat's nose to make the whiskers.

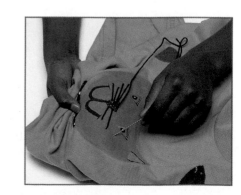

19

Hawaiian Dancer

Aloha! Welcome to a tropical luau. Luau is the Hawaiian word for party and the traditional dress for a luau dancer is a grass skirt with a lei around her neck. Put flowers in your hair to do the hula dance.

YOU WILL NEED

- Large sheet of card (stock)
- Long, sleeveless, pink T-shirt
- Fabric marker pen
- Container of water
- Fabric paint (yellow, pink, orange, red, white, green)
- Fine and thick paintbrushes

1 Insert a piece of card (stock) in the body of the T-shirt. Use the fabric marker pen to draw the outline of the lei of flowers, navel and grass skirt on to the front of the T-shirt.

2 ► Use the fine brush to paint the lei of yellow, pink, orange and red flowers. Add some white to these colours to make lighter shades. Wash your brush each time you use a new colour. Allow the paint to dry.

3 To paint the grass skirt, use the thick brush and different shades of green fabric paint. You can make different shades of green by adding yellow or white paint.

4 ► To make the navel, use the fine brush and pink fabric paint. Allow the fabric paint to dry.

5 ► Turn the T-shirt over. Use the marker pen to draw the outline of the lei of flowers and the skirt. Paint these as before. Now you are ready to hula!

Space Trekker

Go where no other T-shirt has gone before. The fluorescent yellow after-burners on this T-shirt will be seen by aliens in all the far-flung galaxies.

YOU WILL NEED

- Large sheet of card (stock)
- Dark, short-sleeved T-shirt
- Chalk fabric marker
- Container of water
- Fabric paint (dark blue, light blue, black, red, fluorescent yellow, silver)
- Medium and thick paintbrushes
- Iridescent fabric paint (red)

1 ► Insert pieces of card (stock) in the body and sleeves of the T-shirt. Use the chalk fabric marker to draw outlines of planets and stars. Draw the end of the rocket and its thrusters.

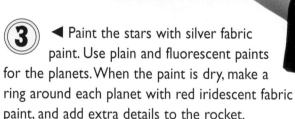

2 Paint the rocket with dark blue, light blue, black and red fabric paint. Use fluorescent yellow fabric paint for rivets and the glow of the afterburners. Paint the top of the rocket silver.

3 ◄ Paint the stars with silver fabric paint. Use plain and fluorescent paints for the planets. When the paint is dry, make a ring around each planet with red iridescent fabric paint, and add extra details to the rocket.

4 To make galaxies of stars, dip the thick brush in yellow fluorescent fabric paint and flick the brush at the T-shirt. Droplets of paint will scatter all over it. Repeat until the T-shirt is aglow with dazzling stars. Let the paint dry before starting the next step.

5 ◄ Turn the T-shirt over, making sure that the pieces of card are still in position inside. Use the chalk fabric marker to draw the front of the rocket so that it lines up with the section on the front. Paint and decorate the rocket and the galaxy of stars as before.

Fruity T-shirt and Shorts

This outfit is perfect for the summer, when the sun is shining and it's nice and warm outdoors. Your friends will be so impressed by your new outfit they will be wondering where you bought it!

YOU WILL NEED

- Short-sleeved T-shirt
- Old paper
- Fabric inks
- Fabric ink pads
- Strawberry stamp
- Watermelon stamp
- Shorts
- Iron
- Paper towel

1   Lay the T-shirt flat on a covered work surface with a piece of old paper inside it. This will prevent the print from going through to the other side of the T-shirt and making a mess.

2   ▼ Using fabric ink and an ink pad, print strawberries all over the front of the T-shirt. Print some watermelons in the spaces between the strawberries. Leave the inks to dry thoroughly before trying on the T-shirt.

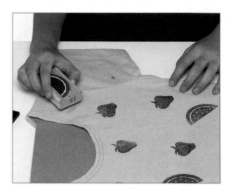

3   ▼ Place your shorts flat on the work surface and put pieces of paper inside the legs. Print strawberries round the legs. Remember to re-ink the stamp from time to time.

4   When the ink has dried on both the T-shirt and shorts, ask an adult to iron them for you (with a paper towel under the iron) to set the ink.

22

Flower Power Leggings

Decorate a plain pair of leggings with lots of different flowers. You can use colours that blend in or contrasting colours that match a T-shirt.

YOU WILL NEED

- Old paper
- Plain-coloured leggings
- Fabric ink
- Fabric ink pads
- Flower and leaf stamps
- Iron

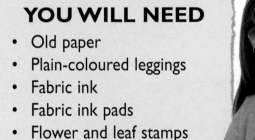

1 ▶ Cover the surface that you are working on with some paper. Lay the leggings flat on the surface. Put a piece of paper inside each leg and at the top.

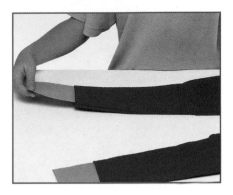

2 ◀ Using fabric ink and an ink pad, print flowers on the leggings with the stamp. Remember to print all over the fabric, because when you have the leggings on they will stretch and the flowers will spread out.

3 ▶ Using fabric ink, print some leaves in a contrasting colour between the flowers. Leave the ink to dry.

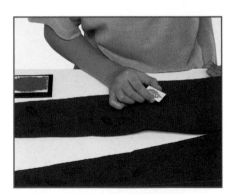

4 ▶ Ask an adult to iron over the stamps to set the ink. After that the leggings are ready to wear!

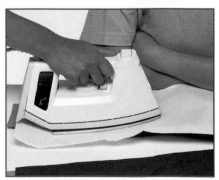

Scraps of felt, beads, buttons and colourful threads can be used to brighten up scarves, gloves and hats. Or use stamp motifs to add some fun designs to your shoes and socks.

Fashion Accessories

Appliquéd Scarf

Winter can be dark and dreary, so why not brighten things up by adding colourful patches to an old scarf. Experiment with any shapes and colours you want, creating a scarf that will be the envy of all your friends!

YOU WILL NEED

- Orange, blue, yellow and pink felt
- Fabric marker pen
- Ruler
- Scissors
- Pencil
- Thin card (stock)
- Plain scarf
- Dressmaker's pins
- Embroidery needle
- Bright, thick cotton thread

1 ▼ Cut six squares from orange and blue felt. Then cut six circles from yellow and pink felt. Cut six smaller circles from blue and green felt.

2 ▼ Draw a flower pattern on a piece of thin card and cut it out to make a template. Make six flowers by drawing around the template on scraps of felt. Cut them out.

3 ▼ Pin three squares to each end of the scarf and sew in place. Sew large circles on top. Place a flower and small circle in the centre. Secure with small stitches.

Wintry Gloves and Scarf

This designer set of accessories is sure to keep those chilly winds at bay in wintertime, and no one else will own such an eye-catching set. You could make these as a special Christmas present for your friends or family.

YOU WILL NEED

- Thin card (stock)
- Pencil
- Scissors
- White and different coloured felt
- Fabric scissors
- Plain scarf
- Pins
- Sewing needle
- Embroidery thread
- Small glass beads
- Mini pompoms
- Plain gloves

(1) Using a template made of card (stock), cut out the snowman's head and body from white felt. Pin the snowman to one of the ends of the scarf and sew him on.

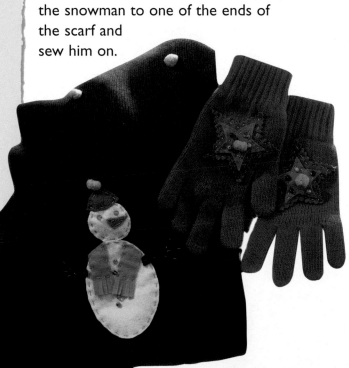

(2) ▼ Cut the carrot nose, hat, scarf and arms out of different coloured pieces of felt. Position the shapes on the snowman. When you are happy with the shapes, pin them and sew them in place. Sew a few beads down the front of the body for buttons and two on the face for eyes.

(3) Sew a mini pompom on the tip of the hat. Sew more pompoms around the snowman and over the scarf to look like little snowballs.

(4) ▼ For the gloves, cut two large and two small stars out of felt. Sew one large star on to each glove. Sew the small stars on top of the large ones. Sew on beads and a pompom.

Fancy Gloves

Why not brighten up your winter gloves with this puppet family? Their hair is made from coloured cotton, and their faces are beads and buttons.

YOU WILL NEED

- Thick blue and green thread
- Darning needle
- Pair of plain gloves
- Scissors
- Thin satin ribbon
- Fine felt-tipped pen
- Felt scraps
- PVA (white) glue
- Small beads and buttons

1 ► Sew loops of blue thread into the top edge of the little finger. Make a small stitch after each loop to secure it. Sew long loops of green thread into the top edge of the third finger. Make a small stitch after each loop to secure it.

2 Snip the ends of the loops and trim the thread. Plait the green thread and tie the ends with ribbon.

3 ▼ Draw the hair, the bow-tie and all the other shapes on scraps of different coloured felt using the felt-tipped pen. Cut them out.

4 ◄ Glue the felt shapes to the front of the fingers, using PVA glue. Leave them to dry.

5 Arrange all the beads and buttons on the puppets, and glue them in place. Let the glue dry thoroughly before you play with your glove puppets.

Pompom Hat

Beat the cold with this fun pompom hat made from an old pair of wool tights. The pompoms are made from leftover balls of wool. The hat looks so stylish that no one will be able to guess what it is made from.

YOU WILL NEED

- Pair of wool tights
- Measuring tape
- Scissors
- Darning needle
- Thin wool
- Pencil
- Pair of compasses
- Thin card (stock)
- Knitting-wool remnants

1 ► Measure 15cm (6in) down from the top of each leg of the tights. Cut off the legs and discard.

2 Thread the needle with wool and sew along the top of the cut ends. Put it tight and sew two more stitches to keep the ends gathered. Cut the thread.

3 ► Draw two circles with the pencil and pair of compasses on the card. Draw two smaller circles inside. Cut out the larger circles. Ask an adult to cut out the smaller ones.

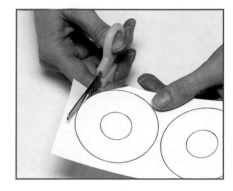

4 Place the circles together. Tie the end of a length of wool around them. Wrap the wool around the circles, passing it through the central hole until it is filled in.

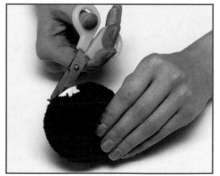

5 ◄ Snip through the wool at the edge of the circles. Pull the circles slightly apart and tie a piece of wool around the centre between the circles, to keep it all together. Pull the circles off and trim any uneven wool.

6 Make a second pompom in the same way. Sew each pompom to one end of each gathered leg. Roll up the waistband a couple of times to make a brim, and tie the legs loosely together to wear the hat.

Stamped Scarf

You can wear this fun scarf around your neck or tied round your head. You could make your own scarf to print on by cutting out a square piece of plain fabric, folding over the edges and sewing them down.

YOU WILL NEED

- Old cloth or paper
- Large white scarf or piece of fabric
- Fabric inks
- Fabric ink pads
- Stamps
- Iron

1 ► Cover the surface you are working on with an old cloth or paper. Spread the scarf or fabric flat and stamp an image in each corner.

2 ► Stamp different motifs around the edge of the scarf.

3 ◄ Scatter more motifs in different colours in the middle of the scarf and leave the inks to dry.

4 ► When the inks have dried, place an old piece of cloth on an ironing board and place the scarf on top of it with the right side facing down. Ask an adult to iron it all over to set the inks.

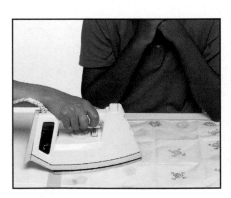

5 When you choose the ink colours for your stamps, try to match them to some clothes you already have so that you can team up your new scarf with your wardrobe.

Bug Socks

Shock your friends with these creepy-crawly socks. Remember to use cotton socks so that you can iron them to set the ink.

YOU WILL NEED

- Old cloth
- Plain coloured socks
- Fabric ink
  - Fabric ink pad
  - Bug stamps
    - Iron

1 ▶ Cover the work surface with an old cloth and lay the sock flat. Print the spider all over the socks. Print smaller bugs around the spiders. When the ink is dry, turn the socks over and do the same to the other side.

2 ◀ Print on a different coloured pair of socks and you can wear odd socks.

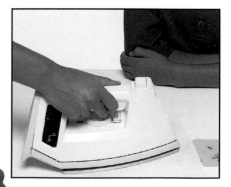

3 ▲ When the ink has dried, ask an adult to iron each sock under a paper towel to set the ink.

31

Doodle Print Shoes

Give a pair of shoes a new look by printing fun all over them. You could also replace the plain shoelaces with bright pieces of ribbon to add an extra splash of colour.

YOU WILL NEED

- Plain coloured gymshoes
- Newspaper
- Fabric inks
- Fabric stamp pads
- Set of doodle stamps
- Fabric glitter glue
- Ribbon

1 Fill each gymshoe with some scrunched-up newspaper. Press it in quite firmly. This will make the shoes easier to print on.

2 ▼ Print the doodle stamps on the shoes, pressing gently. It may help if you slip one hand in behind the spot where you want to stamp. Leave to dry.

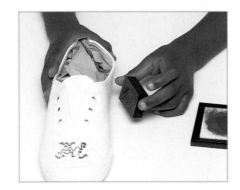

3 ▼ Decorate the shoes with fabric glitter glue in funny shapes or small spots.

4 ▲ Thread a brightly coloured piece of ribbon through the lace holes of each shoe. They are now ready to try on and dance in.

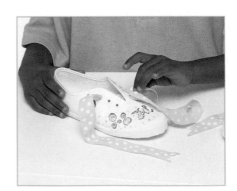

Sunglasses Strap

This sunglasses strap is very useful and a lot of fun to wear. When you do not want to wear your sunglasses, you can hang them around your neck. You could make sunglasses straps for all the members of your family or as gifts for your friends.

YOU WILL NEED

- Stranded embroidery thread
- Scissors
- Electrical tape
- 2 jewellery clamps
- Pliers
- 2 metal rings
- 2 rubber sunglasses attachments

1 Cut six strands of thread, each measuring 2m (6ft) long. Knot the threads together, 5cm (2in) from the top. Tape them to the work surface. Take the red thread and put it over the other threads, then under them and through the loop. Pull the thread tightly. Continue until you have as much as you want of that colour and want to change it.

2 ▲ Take a new thread and continue knotting in this way and changing the thread colour as often as you wish.

3 ▲ When the knotted cord is about 70cm (2ft) long, tie the threads in a tight knot close to the braid. Trim the loose threads very close to the knot at each end.

4 Attach a jewellery clamp over each knot and close the clamps. Attach a metal ring to each clamp and a rubber loop to each ring. To attach the strap, thread the rubber loops over the arms of your sunglasses and tighten the loops around the arms.

33

Clay Fish

This clay fish is really colourful and is guaranteed to brighten up any outfit.

YOU WILL NEED

- Card (stock)
- Pencil
- Scissors
- Self-hardening clay
- Ruler
- Rolling pin
- Modelling tool
- Acrylic paints
- Paintbrush
- PVA (white) glue and glue brush
- Badge pin
- Electrical tape

1 ▶ Draw a fish on the card (stock) and cut it out. Don't forget the fins and tail. Roll out a piece of clay slightly bigger than the fish and about 5mm (¼in) thick. Place the cut-out on the clay and cut around it using a modelling tool.

2 ◀ Mark features and some patterns on the fish with the sharp point of a modelling tool. When you have decorated the clay, leave it to harden in a dry place overnight.

3 ▼ Paint the fish with bright colours. Don't forget to paint the back of the fish. Let each colour dry before painting over it.

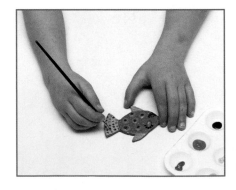

4 When the paint is dry, glue the badge pin on to the back of the fish. Let the glue dry before securing the badge pin with electrical tape.

Papier-mâché Cat

Watch this cat's eyes twinkle under bright lights. The gemstones used for the eyes can be purchased at most art and craft stores. Paint the cat's face whatever colour you like, with a different colour for the ears.

YOU WILL NEED

- Card (stock)
- Pencil
- Scissors
- PVA (white) glue and brush
- Newspaper
- Acrylic paints
- Paintbrush
- Scrap of felt
- Artificial gemstones
- Pipe cleaners
- Button
- Badge pin
- Electrical tape

1 Draw a cat's head on card (stock) and cut it out. Add water to the glue to make a runny paste. Tear the newspaper into small pieces. Put the paper into the paste and then on to the cut-out cat's head. Do three or four layers. Leave overnight in a warm place to dry and harden.

2 Paint both sides and allow to dry. Varnish the front with a mixture of white glue and water.

3 Cut out two felt triangles and glue them on the cat's ears. Glue on two gemstones for the eyes. Cut three pieces of pipe cleaner about 5cm (2in) long and glue them on to make whiskers.

4 ▲ Glue a button on to the centre of the pipe cleaners for the cat's nose. Hold it in place for a few minutes until the glue holds.

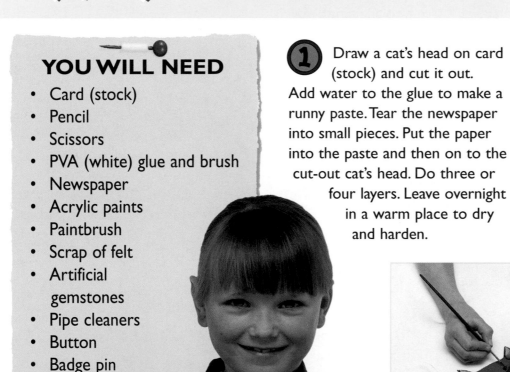

5 ◄ Paint eyelashes around the eyes and paint a thin line around the felt ears.

6 Glue the badge pin on to the back of the cat's head, toward the top of the head. Leave to dry. Secure the pin with electrical tape before trying on your badge.

Birthday Badge

What could be a better present for one of your friends than a personalized birthday badge? Make whatever number you need.

YOU WILL NEED

- Paper
- Pencil
- Scissors
- Rolling pin
- Home-bake modelling clay
- Ruler
- Modelling tool
- Biscuit cutter
- PVA (white) glue and brush
- Badge pin
- Electrical tape

1 Draw your chosen number on a piece of paper and cut it out.

2 ▼ Use a rolling pin to roll out a piece of clay to about 5mm (1/4in) thick. Place the cut-out number on it and cut around it using a modelling tool.

3 Roll out a piece of clay in a contrasting colour to the number and cut out shapes, such as a star, using a biscuit cutter. Stick the stars on the number with glue.

4 ► Decorate the number with the modelling tool. Put it on to a baking sheet. Ask an adult to bake it in the oven following the clay manufacturer's instructions.

5 When the badge is cool, glue the badge pin on to the back. Let it dry before securing with electrical tape.

Button Heart

This badge makes a terrific present for someone special on Valentine's Day.

YOU WILL NEED

- Card (stock)
- Pencil
- Scissors
- Acrylic paint
- Medium paintbrush
- Buttons
- PVA (white) glue and brush
- Ribbon
- Coloured tape
- Thread
- Needle
- Badge pin

HANDY HINT
When buying card for your badge, make sure you choose some that is thin enough to cut with scissors, yet stiff enough to stand up straight when all the buttons are glued on.

1 ▶ Draw a heart shape on a piece of card. Cut it out and paint it on both sides.

2 ▼ When the paint has dried, glue the buttons on to one side.

3 Tie a piece of ribbon 25cm (10in) in length in a bow. Glue the two ends of the ribbon on to the back of the heart. Let the glue dry. Stick a piece of coloured tape over the ribbon.

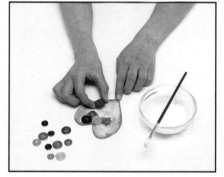

4 ▼ Sew the badge pin on to the back of the ribbon bow. Ask an adult to help you, if you find this too hard.

Happy Face

Brighten up your day by wearing this smiling badge. Hair made out of pipe cleaners gives it a really wacky look.

YOU WILL NEED

- Card (stock)
- Pencil
- Ruler
- Pair of compasses
- Scissors
- Felt
- Felt-tipped pen
- Double-sided tape
- PVA (white) glue and glue brush
- Fabric paints
- Fine paintbrush
- Coloured paper
- Badge pin
- Electrical tape

1 Draw and cut out a circle 12cm (5in) wide on card using a pair of compasses. With a felt-tipped pen, draw a circle on felt, 1cm (¹/₂in) bigger than the card circle. Cut out the felt circle. Use double-sided tape to stick the card circle on the felt circle.

2 ▶ Make cuts in the felt border around the card circle. Fold over the snipped pieces of felt on to the back of the card and glue them down.

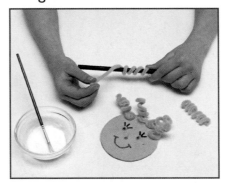

3 Cut out two ovals of felt for the eyes and glue them on. Paint on a nose and mouth.

4 ◀ Coil some pipe cleaners around a pencil to make them curly. Stick on the head.

5 Cut a piece of coloured paper the same size as the face, and glue it on to the back. Glue the badge pin on to the back of the card behind the top of the face. Let the glue dry before securing the pin with electrical tape.

Paper Flower

This paper flower is a great way to jazz up any outfit, but be careful, as it will tear easily. You could make more flowers in different colours and join them to make a bunch.

YOU WILL NEED

- Thin card (stock)
- Pencil
- Scissors
- Coloured crêpe paper
- Pair of compasses
- Pipe cleaner
- Green felt
- Ruler
- PVA (white) glue and brush
- Felt-tipped pen
- Fabric paint
- Needle
- Thread
- Badge pin

1 ▶ Draw a flower on thin card and cut it out. Use this template to cut out three pieces of different coloured paper. Make a hole in the centre of each flower, then thread the pipe cleaner through each one. Coil up the ends.

2 ◀ Scrunch the flower a little to make it look more natural. Cut a strip of felt 20cm (8in) long and 2.5cm (1in) wide. Brush glue on to one side and stick one end on to the flower stem. Wrap the rest of the felt around the pipe cleaner.

3 ▶ With a felt-tipped pen, draw two leaf shapes on the felt. Cut out and glue them either side of the flower stem. Let the glue dry, then paint on leaf veins.

4 With adult help, sew the badge pin on to the top of the stem.

Dressing up your clothes with jewellery is a good way of creating an individual style. Make yourself a colourful bead necklace or thread bracelet, or try a glitzy brooch and earrings.

Jazzy Jewellery

Rolled-paper Beads

These colourful beads are made from the pages of a magazine, but no one will guess when you wear them.

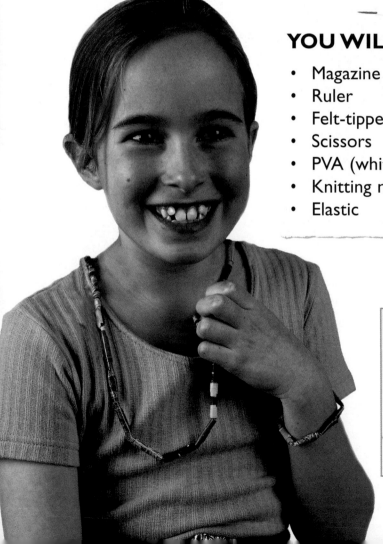

YOU WILL NEED

- Magazine pages
- Ruler
- Felt-tipped pen
- Scissors
- PVA (white) glue
- Knitting needle
- Elastic

1 ▼ Draw lots of 2.5cm (1in) wide strips on the back of the cut-out magazine pages. Make a mark halfway along one short edge of each strip. Draw lines from the two opposite corners to the marked point, dividing the strip into three long, thin triangles. Cut out the shapes.

2 ▼ Starting at the bottom of each triangle, roll the strips of paper around a knitting needle. Roll them neatly, so the bead is even and the edges are neat.

3 ◄ Put a little glue on the end of the paper. Wrap the end over the bead and press it down. Leave the bead on the knitting needle until the glue is dry. When you have enough beads, thread them on to elastic and knot the ends.

Leafy Jewellery

Use leaves and other natural "textures" to make some stunning jewellery. These pieces are very easy and are great gifts for your family and friends.

YOU WILL NEED

- Home-bake modelling clay
- Selection of leaves
- Blunt knife
- Silver or gold modelling powder
- Foil dish or tray
- Varnish
- Paintbrush
- Jewellery fittings
- PVA (white) glue

1 Soften the clay between your fingers. Keep pressing it between your fingers until you have made it into a thin sheet.

2 Place the clay on a flat surface. Press a leaf firmly down into the clay.

3 ▲ Cut the clay around the edge of the leaf with a blunt knife.

4 Lift off the leaf. Then lift up the clay and twist to shape it into a natural leaf shape. Make a hole through the clay with a sharp pencil if you are making a pendant or a key ring.

5 ▲ Dust with silver or gold modelling powder, place on a foil dish or tray, and ask an adult to help you bake the jewellery in an oven according to the clay manufacturer's instructions. Varnish and stick on the jewellery fittings with glue.

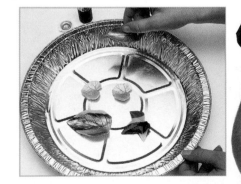

Jungle Bracelet

This bracelet is inspired by the colours you see on an African safari, so it uses brown, orange and yellow threads. If you choose your own theme, such as a rainbow, a sunset or a season, select colours to go with that theme.

YOU WILL NEED

- Embroidery thread
- Electrical tape
- Scissors
- Beads

1 ▶ Cut three brown threads and two orange threads, each 1m (3ft) long. Tie the threads in a knot 15cm (6in) from the top. Fasten the threads to the work surface with electrical tape just above the knot. Lay out the threads, as shown.

2 ▼ Take the brown thread on the left over the orange thread next to it, back under the orange thread, through the loop and over itself. Pull gently to make a knot and repeat.

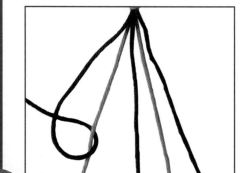

3 Continue knotting as in step 2, making two knots on each remaining thread on the right, until you get to the end of the first row. The brown thread will finish on the right.

4 Take the new orange thread on the far left and make a new row of knots. Continue knotting until it is the right length. Tie the threads in a knot to secure them.

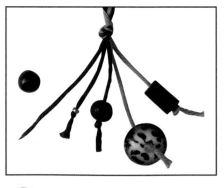

5 ▲ Braid the loose threads and thread a bead on to each thread. Secure each bead with a knot.

Knotty Necklace

Choose your favourite beads to knot into this colourful necklace. If you do not have a jewellery fastener, tie the ends of the threads in a knot.

4 ▼ Make a new row of knots with the new orange thread. After five knots, thread on a bead.

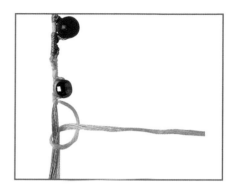

1 Cut four threads, two of each colour and each 150cm (60in) long. Knot the threads 10cm (4in) from the top. Tape them to the work surface above the knot.

2 ▼ Separate one blue thread from the rest. Take it over the other threads, then under them and through the loop. Pull this thread up tightly while holding the other threads.

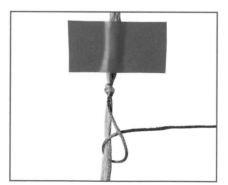

3 After you have knotted a row of about five knots, thread a bead on to the blue thread. Continue to make a few more knots. It is now time to start working with a new thread.

5 Continue making rows of knots and adding beads in this way until the necklace is the length you want. Tie all the threads together in a knot.

6 ▼ Trim the threads close to the knot at each end. Attach a jewellery clamp over each knot and a metal ring to each clamp. Then attach half the fastener to each of the metal rings.

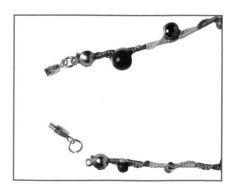

Stripes and Beads Bracelet

This bracelet has beads threaded on to it to add extra sparkle, colour and texture. Use small or medium-size beads, but make sure the holes are big enough for the thread to fit.

YOU WILL NEED

- Soft purple, pink, orange and blue embroidery thread
- Scissors
- Electrical tape
- Small and medium beads

1 ▼ Tie four threads, each 1m (3ft) long, in a knot, 10cm (4in) from one end. Fasten them to the work surface with electrical tape and lay them out, as shown.

2 ▼ Take the purple thread on the left over the pink thread next to it and back under, through the loop and over itself. Pull the thread to make a knot. Repeat to make another knot.

3 ▼ Make knots in the same way on the blue and the orange threads using the purple thread.

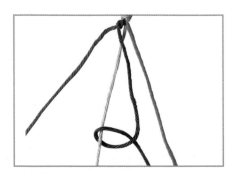

4 ▼ Go back to the new thread on the left, which is a pink thread, and thread a bead on to it. Knot the pink thread following steps 2 and 3.

5 ▼ Go back to the new colour on the left, which is a blue thread. Knot this thread over the first two threads (the orange and purple threads) and, before you knot it over the pink thread, thread a bead on to the pink thread and then knot the blue thread over it. This knot will secure the bead in place.

6 ▶ Continue to knot in this way and thread on more beads until the bracelet is the right length. Tie all the threads securely together in a knot.

7 Braid the loose threads at both ends for about 5cm (2in) before tying knots.

8 ▼ To finish off your bracelet, thread a large bead on to each end and secure with a knot. Trim the ends nearly. Now it is ready to wear.

HANDY HINT
Sort out which beads you need before you start to make the bracelet. It is hard enough keeping hold of the right threads without fumbling in a jar of beads at the same time.

HANDY HINT
If you've never made friendship bracelets before, it may help if you use the same colour threads as in the photographs. This will make it easier to follow the steps.

47

Buttons and Beads

Make some personalized fashion accessories with colourful designs.

YOU WILL NEED

- Home-bake modelling clay
- Toothpick
- Baking tray
- Baking parchment
- Acrylic paints
- Paintbrush
- Embroidery thread
- Rolling pin
- Modelling tool

1 ▶ For the beads, mould pieces of clay to make round, oblong or flat shapes. Pierce a hole through each bead with a toothpick.

2 Lay the beads on a baking tray lined with baking parchment. Ask an adult to help you bake the beads in an oven according to the clay manufacturer's instructions.

3 ▶ When the beads are cool, paint them in lots of different colours and patterns. Allow each coat of paint to dry before adding the next, so the colours don't smudge.

4 ◀ When the beads are dry, thread them on to a piece of embroidery thread.

5 ▶ For the buttons, roll out a piece of clay and cut out small shapes. Use the toothpick to make four holes in each button. Ask an adult to help you bake them.

6 When cool, paint the buttons and allow to dry. Sew them on to your clothes, but don't forget to remove them before washing.

Heart and Star Rings

These rings are great fun and will catch everyone's attention. They are so easy to make, you will soon be wearing one on each of your fingers.

YOU WILL NEED

- Card (stock)
- Pencil
- Scissors
- Home-bake modelling clay
- Rolling pin
- Modelling tool
- Baking tray
- Baking parchment
- Fine sandpaper
- Acrylic paints
- Paintbrush
- Varnish
- PVA (white) glue
- Metal ring attachments

1 Draw a heart and a star on a piece of card and cut them out to make templates.

2 ► Roll out a piece of clay to 1cm (¹/₂in) thick. Use the templates to cut out your shapes.

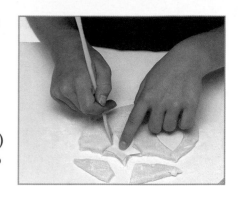

3 Place the shapes on a baking tray lined with baking parchment. Ask an adult to help you bake the beads in an oven. When the shapes are cool, smooth any rough edges with a piece of fine sandpaper.

4 ► Paint the shapes with your own designs, using acrylic paints. Let each colour dry before adding another. When dry, apply a coat of varnish.

5 ▼ Glue a ring attachment on to the back of each shape and allow the glue to dry before trying on the rings.

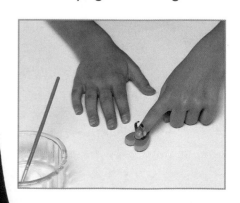

Christmas Tree Earrings

These festive earrings will certainly make you stand out at a party. They clip on, so you don't even have to have pierced ears to wear them.

YOU WILL NEED

- Card (stock)
- Felt-tipped pen
- Scissors
- Gummed tape
- Gold paint
- Paintbrush
- Foil paper in various colours
- PVA (white) glue
- Sequins
- Sewing thread
- Strong glue
- Clip-on earring findings

1 On a piece of card, draw two small Christmas trees and two circles. Cut them out.

2 ▶ Tear up small pieces of gummed tape and dampen the back of them to make them sticky. Stick them on to the circle and Christmas tree shapes.

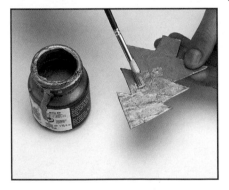

3 ◀ When dry, paint the shapes gold. Leave to dry. Cut out a tree shape slightly smaller than the card tree from the coloured foil. Glue on to the card tree.

4 ▶ Add the decorations to the tree by gluing on a few sequins. Ask an adult to help you make a small hole at the top of the tree and at the edge of the circle, using the tip of a pair of scissors.

5 Thread a piece of thread through the hole in the circle and the hole in the tree. Tie the threads together with a small knot. Using strong glue, stick an earring finding on to the back circle part of each earring. Let the glue dry before trying on the earrings.

50

Star Brooch and Earrings

This glitzy brooch gleams with shiny beads. Why not make a pair of earrings to match it? The earrings are just as easy to make as the brooch, but do not forget to make two!

YOU WILL NEED

- Card (stock)
- Pencil
- Scissors
- Self-hardening clay
- Rolling pin
- Modelling tool
- Beads
- Strong glue
- Paintbrush
- Felt
- Felt-tipped pen
- Jewellery pin
- Clip-on earring findings

1 Draw a large star and two smaller ones on a piece of card. Cut them out.

2 ► Roll out some clay 3mm (¹/₈in) thick. Place the stars on the clay and cut around them. Press beads on the clay stars to make a pattern.

3 ► Paint glue over the beaded stars. This will help seal the beads in the clay and give the stars a smooth finish. Set the stars in a warm place to dry. The clay will harden in about 24 hours.

4 ▼ Place the templates on felt, draw around them and cut them out. Glue the felt stars to the back of the brooch and earrings. Glue on the jewellery pin and clip-on earring findings to the felt. Leave to dry.

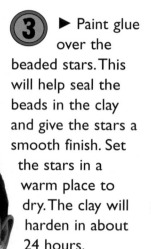

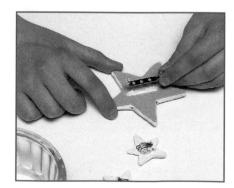

Dressing your hair is such fun, and you'll be surprised how easy it is to make colourful hairbands, headbands, barrettes, scrunchies and slides. Mix and match your colours to go with your favourite clothes.

Funky Hair

Sponge-flower Hairband

Here's a new way of using washing-up sponges. Pink, yellow and green sponges make a flower to decorate and brighten up a plain hairband.

YOU WILL NEED

- Tracing paper
- Pencil
- Thin card (stock)
- Scissors
- Yellow, pink and green washing-up (dishwashing) sponges
- Thin black felt-tipped pen
- Darning needle
- Yellow, pink and green or blue embroidery thread
- Hairband

1 Draw shapes for the petals, the flower centre and the leaves on a piece of card. Cut out the shapes to make templates.

2 ◀ Place the petal templates on the yellow sponge, the flower centre on the pink sponge and the leaves on the green sponge. Draw around the templates using the felt-tipped pen and then cut out the shapes.

3 Place the pink flower centre in the middle of the petals. Sew the centre to the flower with three or four small stitches, using pink thread.

4 ▶ Place the leaves, pointing outwards, on the front of the hairband. Sew the stems to the band with blue or green thread. Lay the flower on top of the stems, and sew its centre and edges to the band with yellow thread.

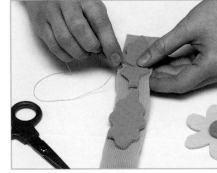

Hippy Headband

Dress up as a happy hippy and wear this colourful band around your head. The more threads you use, the wider the braid will be. Why not make a bracelet to match?

YOU WILL NEED

- Stranded embroidery thread
- Scissors
- Electrical tape
- Large beads

1 ▶ Cut 12 lengths of thread, each 150cm (60in) long. Tie them in a knot 15cm (6in) from the top of the threads and fasten them to your work surface with a piece of electrical tape just above the knot.

2 ▶ Divide the threads into three groups, each with four threads. Braid the threads until the band is long enough to fit your head.

3 ▼ Tie the threads at the end of the braid in a knot. Remove the tape.

4 ▶ Thread beads on to both ends of the headband and secure with knots. Thread another bead on to each end and tie another knot. To make a bracelet to match, cut 12 threads, each 50cm (16in) long, and follow steps 1 to 4.

Striped Beaded Barrette

This hair slide is really useful and looks great with any hairstyle or length of hair.

YOU WILL NEED

- Soft embroidery thread
- Scissors
- Electrical tape
- Small and medium beads
- PVA (white) glue
- Plain hair slide

1 Cut ten lengths of thread, two of each colour and each 80cm (32in) long. Tie the threads in a knot, 15cm (6in) from the top. Tape the threads to the work surface.

2 Take the dark blue thread on the left over the dark blue thread next to it, back under the thread, through the loop and over. Pull gently and repeat.

3 ► Do the same knots on the other threads in the row until the thread you started with is at the end of the row. Go back to the new thread on the far left (another dark blue thread) and repeat the technique explained in steps 2 and 3.

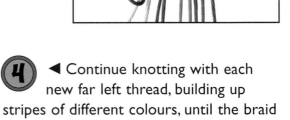

4 ◄ Continue knotting with each new far left thread, building up stripes of different colours, until the braid is the same length as the hair slide.

5 ► Thread small beads on to the end of each thread. Tie a knot on each thread to keep the beads from falling off.

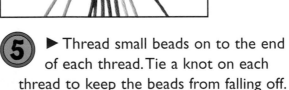

6 Apply glue to the back of the braid and stick it to the top of the hair slide. Fold the knotted end of the braid to the underside of the hair slide and glue.

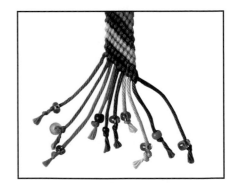

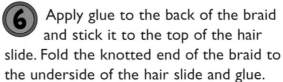

Glitzy Hairband

Create your own designer accessory by sewing an assortment of brightly coloured beads on to a padded hairband.

1 ▼ Cut out some small dots of felt in lots of different colours.

2 ▼ Dab a small spot of glue on to the padded hairband where you want each dot to be. Stick the felt dots on and let the glue dry.

3 ▼ Sew a bead on to the centre of a felt dot. Knot the thread around the bead. Cut the thread as close as possible to the knot. Do the same for the remaining beads.

4 ▼ To make a different style of hairband, select a mixture of beads that matches the colour of the hairband, or create a rainbow effect by sewing your beads in rows of one colour. Use sparkly beads and a plain black hairband to make a special-occasion hairband.

Special Scrunchie

This will make your ponytail very eye-catching. Make it in the same colour as your favourite outfit. For a special occasion, use black velvet fabric and shiny gold or silver beads.

YOU WILL NEED

- Fabric
- Scissors
- Small beads
- Sewing needle and, if available, beading needle
- Sewing thread
- 1cm (1/2in) wide elastic
- Safety pin

1 ► Cut a piece of fabric into a rectangle 30 x 12cm (12 x 5in). Fold each long side of the fabric over to the wrong side by 1cm (1/2in). Ask an adult to iron them flat. Sew a selection of beads on to the right side of the fabric, 2cm (1in) from the edges.

2 Fold the fabric (with the beads on the inside) in half lengthways. Next, stitch the two short edges together, leaving a gap of 1cm (1/2in) in the centre of the edge you have stitched. This gap is for the elastic. Now turn the fabric right side out.

3 ► With the fabric right side out, the beads will be on the outside. Next, fold the fabric horizontally so that the two ironed seams join. Carefully sew around the edge using thread that is the same colour as the fabric you have chosen. To make the fabric scrunch up, cut a length of elastic 40cm (16in) long and fasten a safety pin to one end. Thread the safety pin and elastic through the gap.

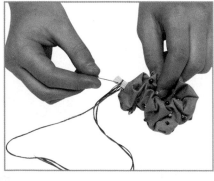

4 ◄ Feed the elastic all the way around until it comes back to the gap. Pull the safety pin out of the gap and unclip it from the elastic. Pull the elastic gently to make the fabric ruffle. Sew the ends of the elastic together. Trim any excess. Sew up the gap with a small slip stitch, using sewing thread that is the same colour as the fabric.

Braided Flips

Braids can be bound tightly with brightly coloured cord for a really unusual style.

YOU WILL NEED

- Comb
- Elastic bands
- Fine cord in two colours
- Hair slides

1 ▼ Comb your hair and part it in the centre. Braid the hair on one side right to the ends. Keep the tension even so that your braid is straight.

2 ► Secure the end of the braid with an elastic band, twisting it back until it is tight enough to hold. Repeat, making a braid in exactly the same way for the other side.

3 ◄ Take a piece of fine cord and, starting at the top, bind the braid by wrapping the cord around it. Keep the circles of cord close to one another.

4 ► Halfway down your braid, you can change the colour of the cord. Hold the end of the first colour against the braid and bind the new colour tightly round it. Continue working right down to the end of your braid, and secure the end of the cord by tucking it into the elastic band.

5 Add two matching slides to either side of your head, at the front or above the braids.

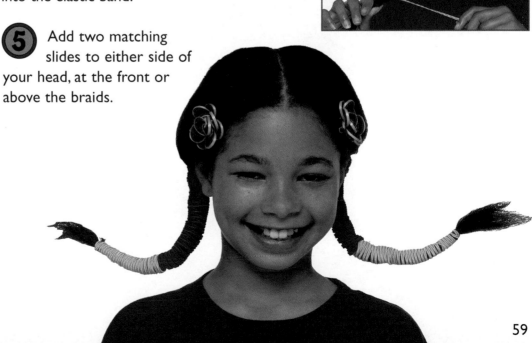

Christmas Hair Slides

These are great presents for anyone with long hair. They are made using neoprene, a light, foam-like fabric that is easy to cut. It can be bought from craft shops.

YOU WILL NEED

- Thin card (stock)
- Pencil
- Neoprene sheets in various colours
- Scissors
- Hair slide
- Strong glue
- Artificial gemstones

1 ▶ Draw a simple Christmas tree shape on a piece of card and cut it out to make a template. Draw around the template on the neoprene and cut out. Repeat to make six tree shapes.

2 ◀ Cut out a scrap of neoprene to fit over the hair slide and fix it in place with strong glue. You might need to hold the neoprene in place while the glue dries.

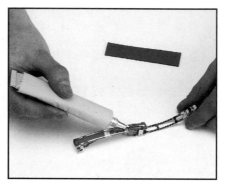

3 ▶ Glue the shapes on the hair slide with strong glue. Allow the glue to dry before trying on the hair slide.

4 ▶ You can also jazz up a plain headband with cut-out neoprene shapes such as stars. Pile on the glamour by gluing an artificial gemstone to the centre of each star.

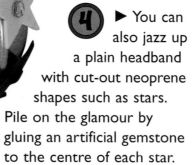

Hair Wrap

These braids look really great! Take it in turns with a friend to do each other's hair. Finish off the braid with beads tied on to the end.

YOU WILL NEED

• Different coloured cotton knitting yarn
• Scissors
• Three medium-sized beads

1 ► Cut three lengths of different coloured cotton knitting yarn, twice the length of the hair you are braiding. Take a 1cm (¹/₂in) section of hair and knot the centre of the threads around the hair, close to the scalp.

2 ► Hold the section of hair away from the head. Select one of the coloured threads and start winding it tightly around the hair and the other threads. The loops of thread should lie very close together.

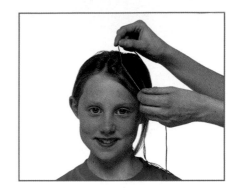

3 ◄ When you have wound as much as you want of the first colour, start winding a thread of another colour in the same way. Keep alternating the colours until you reach the end of the hair.

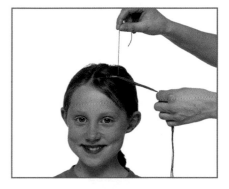

4 ► To finish off, thread a few beads to the end of the hair and tie a knot in the thread to stop the beads falling off. Knot the threads around the hair to stop the wrap unravelling. When you want to remove the wrap, cut off the knot and beads at the end and unwind the threads.

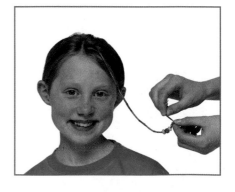

Braiding Fun

Here are some more ideas for braiding your hair using ribbons, cord, glittery thread and beads. To look really great, choose colours that co-ordinate with your clothes.

Be-Bop Braids

High braids like these are easy to do on chin-length or shoulder-length hair. You can twist ribbon around a small section of hair for a really great look!

1 Part your hair in the centre. Take a small section at one side and secure it with a covered band. Twist the band and wrap it around the braid until it is tight. Repeat for the other side.

2 Divide off a small section from one of the braids and slip the end of a ribbon halfway through the covered band. To keep the ribbon in place, tie it on to the band.

3 Twist the ribbon around your hair, tie the ends in a knot and then a bow.

High Ponytail

A high ponytail on top of your head is great for parties and discos.

1 Lean your head forward and brush your hair from the back of your neck to the ends. Hold your hair with one hand and run the fingers of the other hand through your hair to make it smooth. Hold your hair and lift your head up.

2 Put a scrunchie over the knuckles of one hand, then pull your hair through the scrunchie, Twist the band and pull your hair through again. Repeat this until the scrunchie holds your hair really securely.

3 Twist on two more scrunchies above the first one. These will give your ponytail lots of height and make you look tall. To finish, use bobby pins to pin fabric flowers in place.

Beading

Add colourful beads – as many as you wish – to brighten up your hair.

1. Braid a small piece of hair down one side of your face and hold the ends together with a grip. Take a single bead with a large hole and a small piece of glittery thread that you have folded to form a loop.

2. Pass the looped end of the thread through the centre of the bead. Hold the grip on the end of the braid and pass that through the loop of thread. Hold the bead firmly, so it doesn't fall off. Push the bead towards the braid, then pull the ends of the thread. Continue pulling until the end of the braid comes through the bead.

3. Wrap the thread around the end of your braid until you have covered about 1cm ($^1/_2$in) of hair below the bead. Cross over the ends of the thread, then repeat and tie in a knot.

Braids and Bows

Simple braids tied at the back of the head, and tiny front braids decorated with beads.

1. Part your hair in the centre, then take a small section from one side. Start braiding near the roots and work down to the ends. Secure with a covered band.

2. Take a small section of hair from the other side of your head and braid in the same way. Secure with a covered band. Take the braids around to the back of your head. Tie them together with a long piece of ribbon and loop it into a bow. Leave the ribbon ends dangling.

3. Braid two more sections of hair, so that each one hangs in front of an ear. Thread three beads on to each braid and knot them in place.

Crimp Crazy

Big girls use crimping irons to create ripples in their hair, but you can get the same effect by braiding your hair and leaving it overnight to set.

1. Divide your hair into small sections and braid it tightly and evenly from the roots to the ends.

2. Secure the end of each braid with a piece of thread – wrap it around and then tie the ends into a little knot. If you prefer, you can use very small covered beads. Leave the braids overnight to set your hair into its new shape.

3. In the morning unravel each braid, loosening it with your fingers as you go. Comb through using a wide-toothed comb or a brush with widely spaced bristles. Keep your hair away from your face with a coloured hairband.

Index

A

Accessories 5, 24, 40
Acrylic paints 34, 35, 37, 48, 49

B

Badge pins 5, 34, 35, 36, 37, 38, 39
Badges 4, 5, 34, 35, 36, 37, 38, 39
Barrettes 52, 56
Beads 4, 5, 24, 27, 28, 34, 40, 42, 45,
   46–7, 51, 55, 56, 57, 58, 61, 62, 63
Bows 5
Bracelets 5, 40, 44, 46–7
Braids 5, 59, 61, 62–3
Brooches 5, 40
Buttons 4, 24, 28, 35, 37

C

Card 8, 9, 10, 11, 12, 14, 15, 16, 17, 18,
   20, 21, 26, 27, 29, 34, 35, 37, 38, 39,
   49, 50, 51, 54, 60
Chalk fabric marker 11, 21
Clay 5, 34, 36, 43, 48, 49, 51
Combs 5, 59
Cord 59
Crêpe paper 5, 39

E

Earrings 5, 40, 50, 51

F

Fabric glue 10, 12, 13, 16
Fabric inks 22, 23, 30, 31, 32
Fabric marker pens 8, 9, 10, 12, 14, 15,
   16, 17, 18, 20
Fabric paints 4, 6, 8, 9, 10, 11, 12–13,
   14, 15, 16, 17, 18–19, 20, 21, 38, 39

Felt 4, 10, 16, 24, 26, 27, 28, 35, 38, 39,
   51, 57
Felt-tipped pens 26, 28, 38, 42, 50, 54
Foil paper 50

G

Gemstones 35, 60
Gloves 4, 2, 27, 28
Gymshoes 32

H

Hair 4, 5, 52, 54–63
Hairbands 52, 54, 57
Hats 4, 5, 24, 29
Headbands 5, 52, 55
Jewellery 4, 42, 43, 44, 45, 46–7, 48, 49,
   50, 51
Jewellery fittings 33, 43, 45, 49, 50, 51

K

Knitting wool 4, 29

L

Leggings 4, 23

M

Modelling clay see clay
Modelling powder 43

N

Necklaces 5, 40, 42, 43, 45, 48

P

Paint see fabric paints
Papier-mâché 5, 35
Pipe cleaners 5, 35, 38, 39

Pompoms 27, 29
Ponytails 5, 62

R

Ribbons 5, 8, 12, 13, 28, 37, 62, 63
Rings 5, 49

S

Scarves 4, 24, 26, 27, 30
Scrunchies 5, 52, 58, 62
Sequins 50
Shoes 32
Shorts 4, 22
Slides 5, 52, 56, 59, 60
Socks 4, 31
Stamping 4, 22, 23, 30, 31, 32
Stencils 13, 19
Sunglasses strap 33

T

T-shirts 4, 6, 8, 9, 10, 11, 12–13, 14, 15,
   16, 17, 18–19, 20, 21
Templates 10, 12, 18
Threads 4, 5, 6, 16, 18–19, 24, 26, 27,
   28, 33, 37, 39, 44, 45, 46–7, 48, 54,
   55, 56, 57, 62, 63